DEBUSSY

SUITE BERGAMASQUE FOR THE PIANO

EDITED BY WILLARD A. PALMER

AN ALFRED MASTERWORK EDITION

Second Edition
Copyright © MCMXCIV by Alfred Publishing Co., Inc.
All rights reserved. Printed in USA.

Cover art: A detail from View of Heath Street by Night, 1882
by Atkinson Gimshaw (1836-1893)
Tate Gallery, London
Art Resource, New York

...about the
SUITE BERGAMASQUE

by Claude Debussy

The SUITE BERGAMASQUE was composed in the period from 1888 to 1903. The four movements are *Prélude, Menuet, Clair de lune* and *Passepied*. Originally the suite was to have included a *Promenade sentimentale* and a *Pavanne*, as well as the *Masques* and *L'Isle joyeuse*, which were published separately in 1903.

The bergamasque originated in the region of Bergamo, in northern Italy. Frescobaldi used the word "bergamasca" as early as 1635 to refer to a melody used in one of his canzonas, probably a folk tune from the same district. It is believed that the character of the buffoon, Harlequin, was born from a caricature of the humor and the images of the Italian *Comedia dell' Arte*, with its symbolic costumes and masks.

Several of Debussy's works were derived from the Paul Verlaine poem, *Fétes galantes*, which contains a verse entitled "Clair de lune," from which the following is an excerpt:

"... qui vont charmant masques et bergamasques
Jouant du luth et dansant et quasi
Tristes sous leurs déguisements fantasques."

"... they go to charming masques and bergamasques
Playing the lute and dancing and somewhat
Sad beneath their fantastic costumes."

The "masque," as used in these lines, refers to ceremonial social entertainments, a combination of poetry, music, dancing and pageantry. "Bergamasque" implies the use of grotesque attire and clown costumes.

In this suite, Debussy ingeniously and beautifully captures the spirit of these lines in a tribute to the music of the French baroque period, the days of Rameau and Couperin. The form is that of the baroque or classical suite, in which *Clair de lune* takes the place of an aria or one of the slower dance forms.

CONTENTS

PRÉLUDE

The introductory and improvisatory character of the baroque prélude is retained by Debussy. The joyous feeling of this prélude establishes the festive "bergamasque" setting and prepares the listener for what is to follow. The form is more complete than the usual prélude, containing first and second subjects, development, recapitulation and coda. Devices of the baroque period are in ample evidence: appoggiaturas, pedal point, development by episode, etc. This movement contains motifs that are developed in the following movements.

MENUET

The various moods of the menuet are the subject of this movement. It is not confined to "stateliness" or "daintiness," the words commonly applied to the dance. It is, in short, not for dancing but is a free and imaginative treatment, containing the elements of the menuet, charmingly varied and developed by means of fresh and original rhythmic and harmonic subtleties. The classical menuet-trio-menuet treatment is ignored in favor of a concise single movement, consisting of exposition, development, and a short, condensed recapitulation.

CLAIR DE LUNE (Moonlight)

Debussy's most popular work fits like a rare gem into this setting. To hear this movement performed in its proper context may be a revealing experience. The popularity of *Clair de lune* is well deserved. It is highly original, and in this setting it is utterly perfect. It is at once a delicate and luminescent picture of half-light and half-shadow, and a warmly lyrical expression of moods suggested by the title and by the poetic lines that inspired it.

PASSEPIED

The early passepied was written three-in-a-measure. In 17th-century France it was second in popularity only to the menuet. It is gay and rapid in movement. The name "pass foot" is an obvious reference to one of the physical features of the dance. Debussy's *Passepied* is in common time, but more than any of the other movements of this suite, it is reminiscent of the style of the French clavecinists. Like some of the early passepieds, it is characterized by a light, repetitive staccato figure in the accompaniment, which continues throughout the piece. In the suite it serves to restore the festive mood of the opening movement, after the introspective *Clair de lune,* rounding out the work with the logic of form so integral in all the music of Debussy.

NOTES ON PERFORMANCE

Music critics seem sharply divided in their opinions on how Debussy's piano compositions should be played. Some insist the music should have a vagueness which they regard as characteristic of impressionism, while others believe clarity is as important in Debussy's music as in that of any other composer.

The answer is best found in the composer's own opinions. Debussy insisted, according to one of his pupils, Louis Laloy, that there should be no special emphasis on the melodic line or on chords. The music is so written as to make this unnecessary. Those who heard Debussy play spoke of tones that "seemed to be produced without hammers." The words "dim," "veiled," "iridescent" and "transparent" were often applied to his music. Debussy instructed his students to play with sensitive fingertips and to play chords as if the keys were being attracted to the tips of the fingers and rose to the hand as if to a magnet.

Debussy indicated no fingering or pedaling in the *Suite Bergamasque*. The application of the damper pedal is usually clearly indicated by the length of the bass notes. If the use of the third (sostenuto) pedal seems indispensable in this music, it is well to remember that the French pianos of Debussy's day had no such device.

"Overlapping pedaling" must be used frequently. The "half-pedal" is also useful. After a note or chord is played with the pedal down, the foot is lifted slightly so the dampers just touch the vibrating strings without stopping the sound completely. The pedal is then immediately depressed again. This allows the tones to be sustained with considerably less dissonance.

Above all, romantic affectation is to be avoided in this music. Crescendos and diminuendos should never be overdone.

Willard A. Palmer

SUITE BERGAMASQUE

PRÉLUDE

Claude Debussy
(1890)

MENUET

Originally: **pp** *et très délicatement*

Originally: très soutenu

CLAIR DE LUNE

Originally: très expressif

*Originally: peu à peu cresc. et animé

Originally: En animant

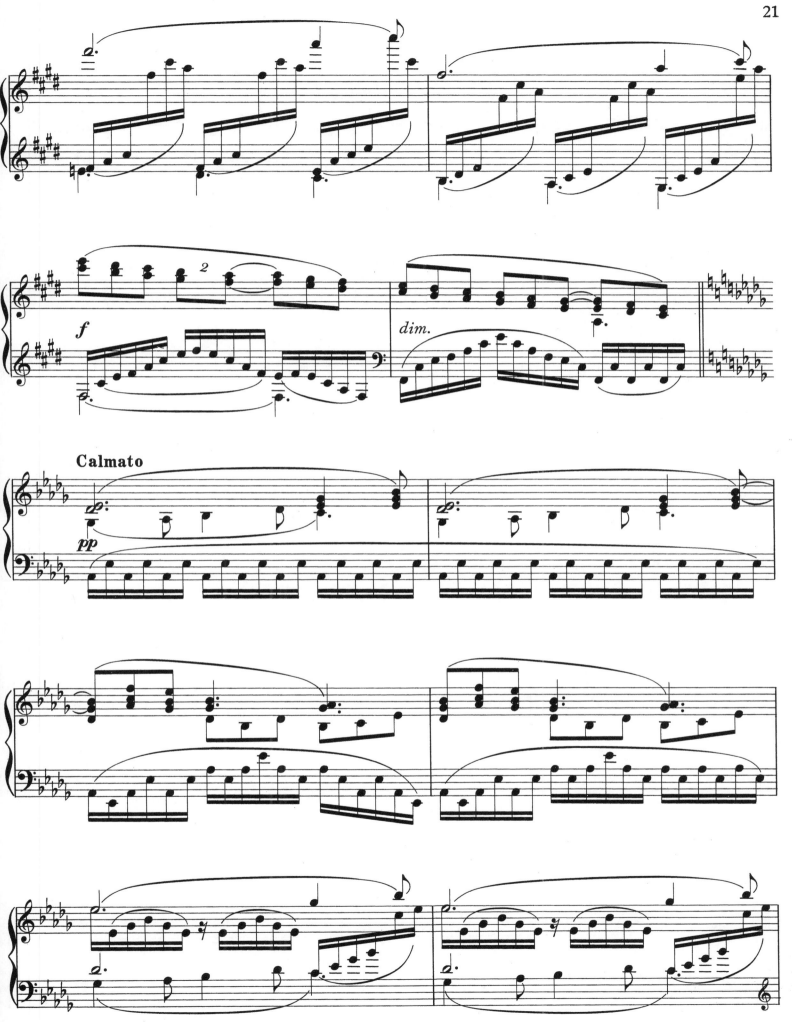

*Originally: morendo jusqu'à la fin

PASSEPIED

Allegretto ma non troppo

*Originally: cédez un peu

slower*.

a tempo

pp

rit.

a tempo

ppp

sim.

ppp

*Originally: cédez